On the Track

D1611978

Written by Andy Seed

Contents

Collins

What's track cycling?

Imagine whizzing around an oval track on a bike, surrounded by other riders, some just millimetres away. Your knees are a blur as you pedal hard, while the watching crowd roars.

Welcome to track cycling.

Fast fact ●●●

Track cyclists can reach speeds of about 70 kilometres per hour!

Track cycling takes place indoors on an oval track, unlike
road racing. The bikes and the races are very different too.

Road racing	Track cycling
● outdoors	● indoors
● on ordinary roads	● on an oval wooden track
● mostly long distances	● mostly short distances
● includes hills	● no hills
● includes corners	● bends instead of corners
● bikes have brakes and gears	● bikes have no brakes or gears

Most track cycling races are held indoors, in a special sports stadium called a velodrome.

Fast facts: the track

- length: 250 metres
- steepest bend: 42 degrees 42°
- made of: 10,000 pine boards
- top speed of riders: 70 kilometres per hour

As the racers zoom around the track, they have to keep between the black and red lines. In some events, the riders travel right up the steep sides of the track. Riders often race very close to each other, which can cause crashes and falls.

Some competitions attract thousands of spectators, who cheer on their favourite riders.

On your bike

If you want to be a track cyclist, you need the right kind of equipment.

Bikes

Track cycling bikes are a lot simpler than road bikes. For a start they have no brakes and no gears!

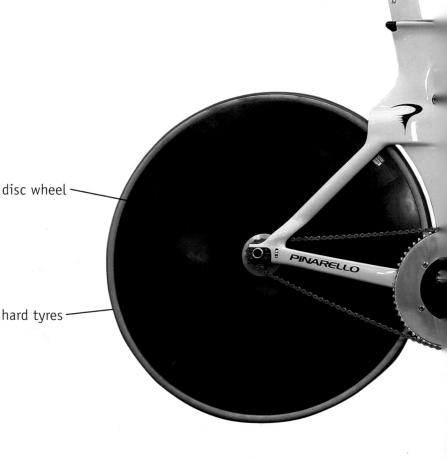

high seat

disc wheel

hard tyres

The pedals are fixed so that riders can't **freewheel**, and the bikes have very hard tyres which produce more speed. Track bikes are narrow to move through the air easily and because riders race so close together.

narrow handlebars

very light **carbon fibre** frame

no brakes

extra-strong forks

no water bottle

no gears

Track gear

Track cyclists wear tight stretchy clothing. This allows easy movement and reduces **drag**. They also need helmets and wear special shoes which attach to the bike's pedals.

Fast fact ●●●

A **professional** track bike weighs about the same as two bricks!

Pedal cleats

These allow the rider's shoes to clip on to the pedals.
Pedal cleats give more power and prevent feet slipping
off during races.

Focus on: Bradley Wiggins

Sir Bradley Wiggins is a hugely successful cyclist both on the road and the track. He's won seven World Championship gold medals, as well as five Olympic golds. In 2012, he became the first British rider to win the gruelling Tour de France road race, an event of nearly 3,500 kilometres. In 2015, Bradley cycled a distance of 54.5 kilometres in an hour and smashed the world hour record.

In the beginning

Track cycling began in the 1870s and soon
became popular. Large crowds flocked to watch riders
on heavy steel bikes racing both outdoors and indoors.
The first World Championships were held in the USA in
1893, and track cycling also featured in the first modern
Olympic Games in 1896.

Over the last 150 years, track cycling has changed in many ways. Tracks changed from slow outside **cinder** or concrete ones to fast indoor wooden ones. Bikes used to weigh up to 12 kilograms but became much quicker to ride in the 1980s when lighter metals were used to make them, followed by carbon fibre in the 1990s.

The types of races have changed too. Women's racing was introduced in the 1950s, and new events have come and gone, including **tandem** races, which featured in the Olympic Games from 1908 until 1972.

Focus on: Arthur Zimmerman

Born in 1869, American cyclist Arthur Zimmerman was the first ever sprint world champion (turn to page 14 for more about the sprint). He won his early cycle races on a **penny farthing**! After learning to race on dirt tracks, Zimmerman became the fastest rider in the world, winning over 1,000 races. He was one of the very first professional cyclists and was once paid in gold when he competed in Europe.

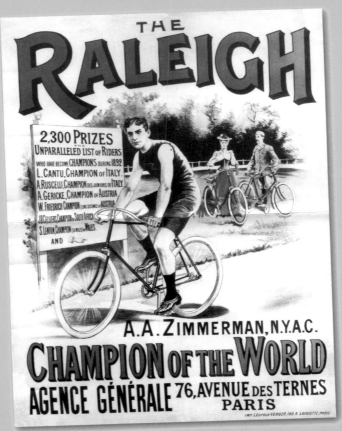

Get set!

Track cycling features lots of different sorts of races and riders – here are some of the best.

Race: the sprint

Two riders go head-to-head to see who can cross the line first after three **laps**. Amazingly, you'll see competitors going very slowly at times (occasionally even coming to a standstill) before an all-out power dash to the finish.

Fast fact ●●●

At the 1964 Olympic Games, two riders kept still on their bikes for over 21 minutes during the men's sprint!

Focus on: Lucien Michard

Lucien was born in France in 1903. A short, stocky man,
he was a great sprinter and was crowned world champion
for four years from 1927 to 1930. In the 1931 World
Championship sprint final, Michard crossed the line ahead
of Willy Hansen, but the judge mistakenly announced
Hansen as the winner and the rules said this had to stand.

Race: the keirin

This is the only race in which you'll see a motorbike on the track! Six or seven riders follow the special motorbike called a derny, and they aren't allowed to overtake it. The derny gets faster and faster, and then it exits the track with 2.5 laps to go, leaving the riders to sprint to the finish line.

Fast fact ● ● ●

The word "keirin" means "fight" in Japanese.

Race: the scratch

The scratch is an **endurance** event of 40 or 60 laps for
15–20 riders, much longer than the fast eight-lap keirin.
The competitors often use the top of the steep track to
launch attacks to get to the front.

Fast fact ● ● ●

Top cyclists spend hours on weight
machines in the gym to help them build
up the extra-strong leg muscles needed
for winning events like the scratch race.

Race: the points race

This is another long-distance event, but this time it's not just about being first past the line – it's about the rider with the most points.

How to win points

- be in the first four in the sprints (every ten laps)
- lap the other riders
- finish first (if it's a tie).

18

Focus on: Erika Salumäe

No one had won an Olympic gold medal for the small
country of Estonia for over 50 years, until 1992 when
Erika Salumäe came first in the women's sprint
race in Barcelona. She'd previously won gold for
the Soviet Union in 1988 and so achieved something
very rare – representing two different countries at
the Olympic Games. Altogether, Erika broke 15 world
records during her cycling career!

Estonia

Race: the individual pursuit

Unlike the points race – which is for a large group of starters – the individual pursuit is for just two riders, each competing to finish in a quicker time than their opponent who starts on the opposite side of the track. The race, which is usually over 3,000 or 4,000 metres, can also be won by catching an opponent.

Race: the team pursuit

This is similar to the individual pursuit but it involves two teams of four riders who start at opposite sides of the track and try to catch each other. The cyclists take turns at the front, blasting around the track like express trains, centimetres from their team-mates.

Pursuit riders use special two-part handlebars to crouch low in races.

Focus on: Laura Trott

Laura Trott is one of the stars of world track cycling, and participates in the team pursuit, **omnium** and scratch race. She's won 20 major championships, despite being born a **premature** baby and suffering from **asthma**. Laura is a professional rider, and even has her own bike clothing range!

Race: the team sprint

This is another team race, but this time each of the two teams has three riders who try to finish in the fastest time. The cyclists take a lap each at the front and then drop out, so only one finishes the race. Riders **slipstream** each other, staying as close as possible to reduce air resistance.

Focus on: Grégory Baugé

This French sprinter is a nine-time world champion and one of the fastest cyclists on the planet.

Baugé has amazing balance and when another rider crashed into him at full speed, Baugé skidded sideways but somehow managed to stay on his bike and finish the event.

Race: the madison

The madison is possibly the strangest race on the track:
a little like tag for cyclists! Teams of two compete for
points over many laps, but even though both riders are
always on the track, only one rider races at any one time –
the riders swap by touching hands.

Fast-forward – racing in the future

Through extensive TV and internet coverage, track cycling has become more and more popular across the world, and this is only set to continue. Increasing numbers of disabled riders are also now enjoying the sport of para-cycling, which has its own championships and Paralympic events.

New technology is making bikes faster, lighter and stronger; new races are being trialled and more velodromes are being built. One thing is for certain: the future of track cycling is an exciting one.

Focus on: Kieran Modra

Australian Kieran Modra is one of the world's top para-cyclists. He is **visually impaired** so rides a tandem with a "pilot" rider who steers and talks him through the race. Kieran has won five Paralympic gold medals and six Para-cycling World Championship gold medals.

Glossary

asthma a medical condition that affects someone's breathing

carbon fibre a lightweight material made up of thin carbon threads, which is used for its strength

cinder lightweight rock that has bubble-like holes, often used for tracks and roads

drag a force, sometimes called air resistance, that slows down moving objects

endurance being able to do something over a long period of time

freewheel roll along on a bike while keeping the pedals still

laps overtake someone by being a whole lap ahead

omnium a track cycling event made up of six different races where riders compete for points

penny farthing an early bicycle with a very large front wheel and a small back wheel

premature something happening earlier than predicted

professional someone who earns money for what he or she does

slipstream ride close behind someone to reduce drag

tandem a bike which carries two riders, one seated behind the other

visually impaired a disability where a person has reduced or little eyesight

Index

The history of track cycling

1870s
track cycling began

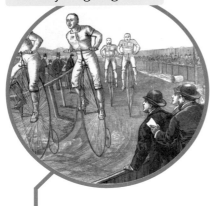

1896
track cycling featured in the first modern Olympic Games in Athens

1870   1880   1890   1900   1910   1920   19

1893
first track cycling World Championships took place in the USA

1908
tandem races were included in the Olympic Games (until 1972)

30

1958
women were included in the World Championships for the first time

1988
women's track cycling was first included in the Olympic Games

0	1950	1960	1970	1980	1990	2000

1980s
lighter metals were used to make bikes, which made them much faster

1996
track para-cycling was first included in the Olympic Games

Ideas for reading

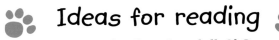

Written by Clare Dowdall, PhD
Lecturer and Primary Literacy Consultant

Reading objectives:
- retrieve and record information from non-fiction
- read for a range of purposes
- identify main ideas drawn from more than one paragraph and summarise ideas

Spoken language objectives:
- participate in discussions, presentations, performances, role play, improvisations and debates

Curriculum links: Physical Education; History

Resources: paper and pencils, ICT

Build a context for reading

- Ask children to talk about any experiences that they have of taking part in cycling activities.
- Look at the front cover and ask children to describe what they can see. Introduce related key vocabulary – velodrome, track cyclist – and ask children to say it and write it.
- Read the blurb to the children and ask for any knowledge about track cycling.

Understand and apply reading strategies

- Turn to pp2–3. Read aloud and ask children to follow, looking for interesting facts that answer the question *What is track racing?*
- Close books and challenge the group to recall as much information to answer *What is track racing?* Make a note of the ideas on a whiteboard, encouraging children to use vocabulary from reading.
- Look at pp2–3 again and add facts to the whiteboard that children find as they reread.